Withering Away In A Respective Collage

Table of Contents

Chapter 1: Withering Away In A Respective Collage 5
    Careless Whispers 6
    Who Am I Now 7
    The Comfort That Exists Within My Glory 8
    I Now Exist 10
    This Futile World 11
    The Menacing One 12

Chapter 2: The Pieces Of Me That Were Within 13
    I Seek Out Justice 14
    The Love I Give Within 16
    The Hidden Passion 17
    Withering Away In A Respective Collage 18
    I Am The Special One 19
    Within My Withered Heart And Soul 20
    Whispers In The Blown Wind 21
    The Beauty Of My Demise 22

Chapter 3: Beautiful Promises, Harmonious Words 23
    Beautiful Promises 24
    You Are The One 25
    With Every Failure Comes Success 26
    I Seek To Write 27
    The sands of time 28
    The Love That Exists Within My Deepened Soul 29
    The place within my heart I so desire 30

    Who Are You Now 31

Chapter 4: The Beauty That I Respect And So Desire 32
    A Beautiful Happy Soul 33
    Our Soul's Journey 34
    Sweet Blessings To Cherish and Explore 35
    Within A Soul Of Beauty And Peace 36
    The Fate of Hope And Glory 37
    How famous people ruined my life 38

Chapter 5: Sacred Words That Exist Within A Kind Spirit 40
    Tomorrow is a better day 41
    The Land's Place 42
    The Night's Journey 43
    The Truth I Bear Will Never Be Known 44
    In Peace I Speak To You 45
    The Light Workers Blessings 46
    The Deep Sorrow 47

Chapter 6: My Soul That I So Cherish 48
    Within My Soul Lies 49
    Sweet Blessings I Once Possessed 51
    My Only Hope 52
    The Empath's Dream 53
    Within My World You Disappeared 54
    Those Who Destroy 55
    I Think I Know You Now 56

A collection of songs and poems about life, love, heartache, beauty and many other facets in life. This collection of poems will entice you and let you feel hope, joy, and let you connect with the words, thoughts and parts of this special tribute. Withering Away in a respective collage will help you feel and heal and will grasp at your very heart strings and allow you to become a part of its very notion and the words that hold dear meaning within.

This collection allows you to flow through the harmony of peace, joy, love and compassion and allows you to become one with yourself and whole. It will give you the solace you desire and let you be in peace with your inner self and speaks to you through it's heartfelt ways. These pieces will speak to you and allow you to flow through their harmonious messages only to bring you back to the place you were meant to be.

Chapter 1:
Withering Away In A Respective Collage

Careless Whispers

Careless whispers in the midst
Set forth my carefree battling ways
Beautiful gestures desired
Bring forth my hasty and wondrous days

Setting forth the times we shared together
Only knowing that you never truly had any idea
Or cared for, the things I ever once desired
Just showing up to make me feel you were inspired

Careless whispers setting forth in the midst
Break free from the battles I face this very moment
Yearning forth the confusion and angst I experience
Times a far in the place of my desired time

Who are you to me any longer
Only a glimpse in my memories own mind
Broken promises oh how you failed me so
Deep with your confused spirit and my precious time

Careless whispers setting forth in the midst
Break free from the battles I face this very moment
Yearning forth the confusion and angst I now deal with
Times come forth in the place of my anguished mind

Who Am I Now

I rush to adore my blessings only to find they've all been lost and gone
Stolen away by the madness that exists the evil we find within an existence and society gone wrong
Where can I find the success I once was the talented creature I once desired to be
With hopes dreams goals and admirations only stolen so I couldn't be free
The memories remain ingrained without a barrier from the past
Only wishing that the goodness and truths be the shining light that would outlast
Within my mind exists a haven for solace and a locale for peace
Only to be engulfed by the burning confusion of the traumas that cannot leave
Who am I now where did she go
Did she just fade away?
Drowning in the madness and misery of a newly created person
One I just cannot get to know
She exists somewhere within
Languishing rushing out through
Crying within the confines of burden she bore reaching out desperately to become heard and known
Who am I now this sorrowful soul
That once was a source of blessings and peace
Stolen promises and memories only existing now as a source of confusion and mercy

The Comfort That Exists Within My Glory

Within my glory lies a comfort that exists
It only grows from the sorrow and aches from the past
It hopes to be let free from a world it knows that it cannot understand
Trying to free itself from the past in a world of confusion lost hopes and angst
Beneath the path of a journey I can only face
Exists and encompasses a world of dreams and freedoms I can only begin to yearn for and imagine
With it draws more hope from the light

The beauty and justice of truth prevails forward and inspires
Hopes and dreams come forth and shine through but little did I know
The world I once knew exists now in a greater space of more peace and comfort
The comfort that exists within my glory
Can never truly be found
It once existed long ago but now has transformed and grown
Into a reality of careless whispers and comfort and freedom I never knew possible
Drowning out the tragedies from the past and the pain that once resided there
Grown into an existence of greater love and pride
Forced to declare and be this strength within every given moment

My deep soul seeks for a way out
My deep soul seeks for a way out
Of this place where I never knew I belonged
It journeyed to an existence I never knew within
Without warning me of exactly where it was going
I had no knowledge of what it stole or that it journeyed far and away
In an existence hoping and trying to pave a different path

It sets forth through
It sets forth through
A yearning and a desire within my deep spiritual mind
A place for sorrows to exist in a disempowered soul
A wondrous place that once was known for her kind

I Now Exist

I now exist within a world I knew not
Tampering with my everyday existence leading to endless fears of sorrow and wrought
My heart sinks deeply for it once hoped for a blessed future
Only to succumb to hopes losses lost goals and confusion
I once sought out the endless hope and truth I so desired
Only to create and exist in a world of let downs and unexpected miseries
Why does my discomfort follow me around so suddenly
Never leaving my side or thoughts
Engulfing every arena of my precious being
Who is the sorrow we avoid and never want to face
While it flicks us in the souls and minds
Every waking second of our experiences

My existence is futile hopes and dreams now lost
Waking every day to a new world and reality
Expecting successes and greatness to appear and suddenly come forth
I create what I believe and reality has sunk in fast
To an expectation I never desired
thwarting the greatness I wanted to last
I now exist in a world and reality i cease to expect
Endless dreams goals and fates confused about their newfound place
My mind an endless confusion of whirlwind my changing fate ever so often being confronted with haste
I now exist in a place deep within my special gracious being and soul marks the place where I need to
exist and generates hordes of blessed scenarios and light rather than distrust

This Futile World

A place full of tragedy and no hope
Sorrows stationary and peace and once glory now lost
Dreams and aspirations can turn into lamented memories of a trodden past
Hoping the future can bring forth change and a greater goodness that forever will last
Your soul suffered many deep tragedies and fates
Only to be blessed with an abundance of gifts and glories you can use to share
Hope somehow paves its way to newfound blessings and joys
Even amidst a writhing world of avid menace and lack of good
Expectations of hope and peace good and series of abundance and blessings
Sometimes to receive nothing but negativity and horrors that create more lack of hope within

I can only surmise that you will continue to pursue on
The hopes and goals that exist deep within your confused still hopeful mind
Expecting extreme success to come forth
With putting forth your dreams and goals and turning them into true success
This futile world once a place of grief and sorrows
Turning into a great land of achievements goodness and greater tomorrows
True glimmers of greatness shining through a slaughtered heart
Marching forward with goodness and grace with no madness or evil that separates or hurts.
A world of love and bliss that which you of all people deserve
Coming forth unlimited abundance and blessings for your amazing soul to live and observe

The Menacing One

Exists deep within the souls of the shattered and the torn
Those who were once whole, pleasant and full of love and joy
Now simply cease to exist in a place full of evil and plummeting
Downward forth towards the spiraling of the corners of my mind
The soul that so exists deep within, ceases to run and love seek and fight
She sighs for towards to the confusion it brings forth
The evils present only bring forth the angst that it so consumes
Only sheds forth the place that it seeks to resume
The love that was once shattered broken confused and worn
Writhes down and around the places that were once whole and good
She seeks to destroy and create discomfort and disharmony
In a beautiful land where precious amazing souls exist
The monster this creation is barely ceases to show mercy
Invading a land it never belonged in or should be a part of
The menacing one the merciless horror monster
Existing in a world of disharmony and lack of peace
She resides within my heart and yearns within my body
Attempting countless horrors and the most loathesome of feats

Chapter 2:
The Pieces Of Me That Were Within

I Seek Out Justice

I seek out justice within the sorrows and traumas emboldened within me
Riddled within a past and reality of confusing worlds selfish dreams and a meddled existence and reality
Where did it all go wherefore does resolution exist
Drowning in endless sorrow while they remain untainted untouched and existing in their own peace
The work of evil committed against an unsuspecting soul
Simple and without the slightest hint of devils or evil within
Unresolved emotions gather deep within sparsed souls
Damaged from a world of once light that existed destroyed within every sense of being
Goodness only was meant to once exist
Replaced relinquished by endless bounds of selfish lack of self-love and hate
Committing atrocities unheard of no remorse sorrow mercy or care as to the lives or lost fate
I seek out justice a soul burning crying out within a reality of what it once was
Hoping that others will pay heed to my endless cries and rush to help out
Unknowing of the reality that I emburden now
The endless deep cries of a broken confused hidden soul
Waiting for the bounds of karma to take effect
wishing courage would draw its way near and within
Allowing the strength that is still stolen
To somehow bravely come forth and make its way through
For if it does prevail the intercessor will be greatly rewarded
By the treasures of truth and happiness that come forth from a once broken healed inner soul
I seek out justice to protect and preserve my very soul life inner core world love and precious being
To be able to exist in a world I once knew before it was broken shattered and stolen

Tainted treasures that yearn to come forth still wallowing in sorrow and heartache
Seek to find truth and resolution to end this harrowing phase of confusion lack of mercy and misery

The Love I Give Within

The love I give within
Is the place of hope I never really found
It's the peace I hold in my own two hands
It's the place I lift within my own self
The hope I've found within my soul
Lies forth within the edges of my own eternal mind
The love I give within, is the place that I can find
The hope that comes forth through, is the peace that I truly need
The love I give within is the place of peace I seek to find
Hope gathers us together in the name of time
Hope is the place I strive to be within in my own given self
I live in a whirlwind of peace and satisfaction
Grave needs mark the heed of my paths desires

The Hidden Passion

I am the hidden passion that resides within me
The deep passion that resides within me cannot be construed
It exists only in a place where I cannot imagine
I belong to my own hidden gifts and talents
In a world full of mercy harmony peace and bliss
The goodness that exists within me cannot be described
For it is the place I seek when I need to understand my current reality and world
My sorrow and misery may still exist within the minor confines of hope
Trying to be released within a soul of peace joy and comfort t
I only hope to find that which can give me an ounce of hope and glimmer
And erase away any madness and negativity that exists deep within
It is a whirlwind of love positivity and and blessings of beauty and light
Riddled with excursions of that which can create maddening amounts of harmony love and unlimited light
Glittered with blessings of joyous abundance existing flying within
Dancing around endlessly creating harmony and blessings of happiness and total abundance
Thoughts of love expressed outwards towards a universe of unlimited greatness
I can only bring forth the blessings that exist within me and transfer it all to others
Giving an outpouring of blessed gifts
The joy experienced within a blessed harmonious soul
The bliss they seek within I give and rush out to them in glimmering hope and abundance
Transforming a once tattered unhappy soul
Into a vortex of love beauty and light
Their souls can now dance too with me as I continue blessing them with goodness and grace.

Withering Away In A Respective Collage

Withering away in a respective collage
I fought to save her soul deep inside
I wished and willed them away so strongly
But yet they remained to steal my goodness and pride
In the middle of the maze, I find myself stuck
Searching for endless ways to Burrough out
Burrowing they did intertwined with those I knew
The sickness possessed i cannot even begin to doubt
Withering away in a respective collage
I fight to save my solemn endless trodden soul
I wished and willed them away so strongly
Yet heartily did they stay to destroy my dreams and goals
Within the great divide I fit to will and seek
Stolen dreams and lives so sickly ruined
I wish to will it all back, or so i may think
It all was taken from me in the blink of an eye
Withering away in a respective collage
I fight to save her being, her heart everything
I tried to remove them from her trodden destroyed life
But they stayed so solemnly mocking it all
Withering away in a world she once knew
Her greatness taken, everything swept away
In madness she fights it all, as they string her along
No mercy they show every hour and each day

I Am The Special One

I am the special one you love and praise
The special one you love and praise
Is the one who holds you near and dear to him
The true one who holds himself near to his soul
The one who calls out to you his tender loving fool
I am the special one you love and praise
Deep within it my beautiful engulfed heart
Stands still in the lands of time it praises the beauty enthralled
Within my trodden love I fill
A place where my heart seeks the lands untouched.

I am the special one you love and praise
The special one you love and praise
Is the one who holds you near and dear to him
The true one who holds himself near to his soul
The one who calls out to you his tender loving fool
I am the special one you love and praise
Deep within it my beautiful engulfed heart

Within My Withered Heart And Soul

Within my withered heart and soul
Lies a deep phased truth that so exists within
The praising of love, beauty and soul
My heart can only praise that which exists inside
A lovingness of care that so desires away the wishes
We hold near and dear to ourselves deep within
Our souls cherish the love we so preciously stave away
That which exists in a futile world the one we so hold
Near and dear to the wishful hearts that exist in our own demise
The love that comes forth through within my hearts desire
I seek to find the battles that come forth through
Only to find the gaping hole within that my soul so aspires
The tattered soul so misshapen, confused and worn
Aspiring through the thickets of the branched trees
Trodden within deep until the offsetting sorrows of my mind
I find myself withering away in the willows of my own goals
Deep farrowing in the shadows of the places of my mind and soul
Pieces of me come gaping through, showing themselves off
In the corners of the wispiness of my shadowy life
Life seems to be the confusing place of my gasped mind

Whispers In The Blown Wind

Whispers come gaping forth in the blown wind
My shattered heart and soul exist in the sorrowful place
Only coming to and fro from a place I never knew
Existing in the mind of a place I once thought I felt
Who is she now, the girl they once knew
The confusion and sorrow comes deep within
The places she only once thought she felt through
The whispering willows exist in the wind that blows
They come forth to and fro to a place she never knows
Her heart laments from a place she once felt instant and great hope
Only shattered and confused now in a place where it doesn't exist anymore
Her confused mind rambling on and on in the midst
Wondering where and how it all went wrong, the turns the twists
Whispers in the blowing wind, come shattering through the night
Clearing the sound of the one who feels fear and fright

The Beauty Of My Demise

The beauty of my demise lies ahead and lays low
Two triggers run amuck deep within the places I run forth
I can only consume that which never truly existed in places my heart had sworn
Careless whispers existed in a world where hearts are shattered and torn
She only exists and serves as a place of constant destruction
Haphazardly acting upon that which is something of great harrow
I never knew the places she ran forth to and fro
Hoping to God she found a safe haven from the creatures that tormented her
Never did she expect the horrors that came her way that very one day
To turn her world upside down into something of extreme confusion and hell
The beauty of my constant and riddled demise
Never should have ever truly existed
Never was it supposed to happen, in a distant world where hatred and evil co-existed
In her shallow confusing world, the place no one believed or cared for
She suffered aguishly hoping for someone to be able to save her
In the land of truly great sorrows, daily she lamented
Expecting help from those who greatly cared for her
The beauty of her demise, only existed
Because of how precious and great her soul was
Otherwise, it can only be construed as
The destruction of a great and precious soul
  As menacing and harrowing as the torment that lies within

Chapter 3: Beautiful Promises, Harmonious Words

Beautiful Promises

Beautiful promises compromised and broken within my mind
Creating great emptiness confusing me deep inside
I find myself withering away in the confines of my desperate soul
With treasures that belonged once to me, gone gone long ago

Expecting the ways of what I should truly be
My inner soul and being confused from the evils being done to me
I perceive myself whispering in the midst of all of this twisted chaos
With the love i once had taken away harshly while i become haughtily engrossed

Beautiful promises that were once part of my aching breathing mind
Stolen from my wonderful life, right before my very confused hurting eyes
A life once lived with great promise, hope and love
Taken away cruelly and mercilessly without a thought or care in the world

My soul they seek to steal, my hearts desire they wish to take
Manifesting the great divide of my life, their grave horrid mistake
They wish to explain the tragedies i live through untold
Unaware of the lack of goodness and the evil they constantly show

Beautiful promises compromised and broken deep within my grieving exhausted mind
Stolen from the gift of the life i once lived and had
Great promises and wishes, taken away with no chance of hope
I only wish i could replace this existence with one of love and good

You Are The One

The anguish I face, the sources I endlessly deal with
Break free from my confused withered self
Set forth the make-up of my current reality
Bringing forth the pleasures and cards i was supposed to be dealt

The sorrows and mercy I ask for go unanswered
The prayers I seek and ask through with confusion and haste
You are the one I ask for help and guidance from
The one I come to when all my problems have been erased

The one I give my heart and soul to, is the place i come forth to
The one I need and desire, is the one who sets my love on fire
The love I so set my life to give every desire to
The beauty I encompassed within my every life's cherishing need
You set me free, when there was no one who cared
Gave me the hope and love I so wished and desired
The love I encompass passes through so deeply blessed
Only hoping for more ambition, hope and good to admire

With Every Failure Comes Success

With every failure comes success
Lamenting a creative heart to pursue
Desires unspoken of talents gifts hidden and unknown
To spark a greater peace and beauty thereof
Out of bounds it seems true greatness and hope where sparks exist
Creating a brighter and greater future of intricate blessings glory truth and light
The hope we speak of trumps true desire
Seeking solace in every word spoken and deed done
Passions United dreams desired
Hope abounds the joys and love we encompass
Where only we hope that the truths come forward
Exalting above the lengths of confusion and fear
Deep within my inquisitive writhing heart and soul
The success of failure lies deep only to be discovered
Trodden down forth the lands of unbearable sorrow
Trying so hard to work it all out, to be the greatest glory
Only to find ourselves lamenting in spaces of confusion
Where failures turn to success turns that confusion upside down

I Seek To Write

I seek to write and bring forth the feelings I hide deep inside
Within my spirit and soul, a place I lurk seeks to abide
My sorrowful soul aching from the demise of my confused presence
Writhing down inward to a place where my life and confusion hesitates
My writing creates a comfort deep within me, a place of solace I never knew existed
For I pause and hesitate bringing intriguing words together
Creating auras, excursions and creations places I wished I were at
Attempting to exist in the glimmer of goodness and hope
Leaning forward in the midst of ideations that have been stolen
The beauty that comes forth through the written word
Media hesitates to bring the shallow ideation of my thoughts
I can only immerse myself in the solemn spoken word
The pieces of me that are finally written down
I seek to write, to ail my aching sorrows
The willows of my wisps barely yearn to find their way through
The standards of once what was, my ever confusing mess
The places where I seek to find a part of me that once was
I seek to exist, where written word matters
The pieces of my confusing heart where it enmeshes
Can only come forth down the land of confusion and solace
A place of my heart and soul where my true spirit exists

The sands of time

The sands of time tell tales untold
With which their beauty and comfort unfold
Existing in a land where hearty baskets open their buckets
Today our futures tell extreme tales untold
We seek to comfort him in a place where his destiny will unfold

I thought I knew the real you
But little did I know you
The grave you I once knew
Ceases to even exist anymore

I now exist in a land where my heart sinks in desire
I read only to exist the thoughts and minds desires
Within it living a land of futile gifts and careless whispers
Sitting only in the presence of a stockyard where I was once known
Now existing in a different land
With many stories and dreams untold
The sands of time hold deep forth
Within the passion of my kindred spirit
I can only hope the grave way deep within finds its shelter out
For the sake of my Godly yearnings and soul's desires
We sit and sink only within the folding of the unknown
Time has come back to haunt our bestowed blessings
We find ourselves inching away from the perils of our needs and wants
Desires that are well unknown find their own way down the trodden path
The places of time once knew a place I justified for my own sake
The unwinding path of love joy peace and hope
Only finds it ways untethered roaming the lands freely of its hope
Coming forth to the place where we existed where our heart was free

The Love That Exists Within My Deepened Soul

The love that exists within my deepened soul
Is the love I so seek to find within myself
The hope that halters forth to and fro
Is the gift of love and life that I so deeply desire
My heart sings kisses and beautiful notes
To the praise that my sorrow brings to forth
Deep inside the trodden path I pave through
Is the place I so seek, that allows me to inquire to
The love that exists within my withered heart
Is the love I so seek to push into the place of my dreams
The hope that halters forth to and fro
Is the gift of joy and peace that lets me sing and preen
A place of virtue I so heartily stand,
Way beneath my hearts desires
The sorrow that laments forth deep within through
Stands forward and sets my solemn mind on fire
I am the love you so seek and desire
I am the person you need deep within and inside
My heart belongs in a place so deep and special
A place where your true self and soul resides
A wondrous place in my soul
Seeps forward with memories that I cannot hide
The beauty that flows within through
Exists in a place that I sit in and derive
I am the existence I so seek and desire
Wondrous memories and treasure to behold and admire

The place within my heart I so desire

The place within my heart I so desire
The wondrous sorrow that aches with my talents fire
Pure kisses beautiful phrases that sing songs forth
Rest assuredly deep within the comfort that troddens to and fro
I am the beauty I so seek deep inside
I am the love I capture within which my heart truly resides
I seek to erase the past of which my futile existence cannot bear
A past of nothing but sorrow and madness
A world in which I could not comprehend to be a part of
A wondrous life in which I could not be incorporated into
Is the life I desired to live by, never existing or getting through
Rest assured, the life I once knew, not the place I thought it was
The place within my heart I so desire
Is not the place I thought I once knew

Who Are You Now

Who are you now
The person within my fragmented tormented mind
Wriggling away my confused frightened self
Shattered dreams that run hither to and fro
Within me you sought a haven for solace
A place to Burrough your trodden minds desires
A shoddy land of fury's enraged
An area for you to shoo away the trellis of fire
The place I once so desired
The land of freedom I once truly despaired
Walking away from the beautiful lands afar
Withered far away to a place I never knew
Who are you now
You seem so far away!
Where on earth did you go?
To where did you furtherly run and stray
We were once truly partners
Partners in a place of games and fun
Then one day it all slipped away
So hard and fast it went running alow
Who are you now?
You were once my one and only
The guiding star to my bright light
The one I loved more than life itself
To aid me through the fright nights
But now you cease to exist
Just a figment of my imagination
Memories from afar derail my very thoughts
Hoping the reality comes true once again

Chapter 4:
The Beauty That I Respect And So Desire

A Beautiful Happy Soul

I am a beautiful happy soul, who seeks forth that which I always desired
I seek to be the great one who lives through my own fruitful intentions inspired
the beauty I possess is one that is encompassed within a great manifest
I solemnly seek out the spiritual guises that exist within my beautiful divine

I am a beautiful happy soul who seeks the pleasure and beauty that i speak of
Desires and wonders set only to set forth the places I can show off
My soul sings songs deeply expecting the goodness that I possess
My soul yearns for the freedoms I once had, the places I desire to be

I am a beautiful spiritual creation who yearns to exist and just be happy
The wonders of my nature come true within the life I desire to live
The grace that has become me exists to being the most patient one
My journey into love, light and harmony has only yet begun

I am a beautiful happy soul, within the confines of love and truth I now exist
Only to be wiped out from the portion of the evils they cannot seem to grasp
The virtues that abound within my beloved blessed spirit
Seek to find a way out, only a place of peace, beauty, love and solace

Our Soul's Journey

Journey into awakening
Awakening to your souls
Inner processes and healing journey as
Is an incumbent part of existing within this world and spiritual world now and forever.
Our souls journey an integral part of our spiritual being only exists to serve our higher selves and the light workers around
Processing endless light energy and goodness elevating the planet around us
Creating an abundance of joy and blessings to all those involved
We seek to bring forth the happiness those lost and so seek
And fortify the concepts of beauty love light and embrace and humble kind and meek
Praising and cherishing goodness and great qualities encouraging blessings of hope and love
Elevating our souls growth levels and seeking help from our higher selves and from the God above
Serving others in need and those in need of it
We work the light of the world and seek to rid the planet of hatred and injustice

Inner healing exists within the core of our beings and can be done through varying modalities and can be accomplished through graven methods of inner peace tranquility and blessing our tragedies and experiences with love and goodness and not allowing them to destroy our inner beings selves or futures.

Sweet Blessings To Cherish and Explore

The blessing we behold can only mask the truth of our true nature within
My soul holds the lies of the beauty and tragedies untold
I faced a whirlwind of sorrows that the gifted never have to ever behold
Again I'm entranced in a situation where my destiny is grappling to unfold
Half-truths mark the mercy of the days that lie ahead
With a hidden past that encases hundreds of deep secrets I never want revealed or to tragically unfold
Predators lurk at every corner begging for my every wish and desire
Seeking only to damage and steal that which was once my beings true love and fire
Hidden wishes deep secrets taken from every corner of my existence
It lurks to steal the solace and comfort I possess and the gifts I consume towards justice
I can only grapple for the feat of my glory and hope that it stays far away
Yet by my presence it awaits and tramples seeking only to embrace and snatch more and more
Sweet blessings I once possessed stolen in a whirlwind of confusion and sorrow
Injustice reeks of my very blood and being in the grips of what I endure tomorrow
Sweet blessings taken and gone without a care in the world
When did it all go away, where did it all go wrong i grapple with the mystery of it all who can I ask for some solace

Within A Soul Of Beauty And Peace

The passion I contain can never be let out
For I am a whirlwind of peace and love happiness within a realm of confusion or hate
I am the justice I seek within me
Searching outwards for something that already exists within me

Greatness exists within a soul of beauty and peace
The harmony led forth allows the soul battles to continue forth
Inclining in form the harmony that sets you free
Existing in a limitless world of passion and freedom

Allowing forth the truths of the world to be set free in an alternate reality or realm
She seeks the freedom she once knew within
A broken tainted soul that replenishes itself with the mercy of hope love and light and

Her greatness sets forth the way to future hopes and goals
Creating abundance in her path in a world of injustice and lack of freedom

She is the calling of hope and justice
The justice I so desire
Transformation within a soul's purpose
Higher love and light and
My love for that which cherishes harmony

The Fate of Hope And Glory

True justices I sought out brought forth my newfound glory
The great alliance brought through the sands of time my newfound fight
The glory I sought out comes forth yonder into the glimmer of hope
The truth that sets me free comes back into the land of the free and brave

My fate once was known yet I barely knew not
The fate I chose for myself was given to me in bits and pieces
It was the vessel that was unknown deep within the place of my heart
I was given a fate I knew not, the time that was chosen for my very life

The glory of the place I once knew not, fallen through lest ye behold
My heart grew fonder as I placed myself in a whirlwind of treasure and hope
The journey that I once knew within my broken heart's fond memory
Was the land of the freedom that I desired to be a part of a true mind

The fate I once knew, was barely known yet I knew not
The glory I chose for myself was not the place of peace or hope that I endured
It was the vessel that was unknown deep within the knowing of my soul
I was given a fate I knew not, the time that was chosen for my very life

How famous people ruined my life

How famous people ruined my life
My world turned upside down
By the temples of their confusion
They constantly churned and chased me around
In the collective place of my world they raided
Empowering me with their godly presence
Showing me they were the ones who were my real true friends
Then flowing around and stabbing me in the back
The fame they held unknown, the fortunes limitless
Never could they ever be the greatest humans they founded
The people who the masses worship, the collectively known
While the media chases them around gaining information for the world
How famous people ruined my life
Claiming they were my only and best friends
Putting me up on a pedestal for the world to show
My soul bounds the confusion they embarked upon
The endless madness of their confused mentality within their musical shows
Useless silliness, the fun we had boundless but with it came a price
They came to me over and over founding a place in my soul they sought to take
Coming over unattended with attempts to claim my piece
The famous people how they ruined my life
Funny gods they were endlessly showing off their expensive merchandise
The collection of autos one had can only be construed as some kind of psychosis
They only wished to be a part of me, the awestruck fan lapsed in confusion
Consistently reprimanding their presence
And asking how they chose me over the others
My world they raided with their egoistic presences
Thinking they were living legends, though yes they were

And I just a random living human
The famous people how they ruined my life
By sitting back as a predator came by swiftly
Knowing the situation of what was to come
Never speaking a word to me or the truth uttering
The famous people I once knew
My true and only close friends
I thought our bond was trodden sealed endless
And we would be together until the very end
The famous people I once knew
Finally ghosted and ran away
Their time had come to move on
It was a very confusing meticulous day

Chapter 5:
Sacred Words That Exist Within A Kind Spirit

Tomorrow is a better day

Tomorrow is a better day
Seeping through the windows of my deep great soul
Within my deep great sorrows, I seek
A mindful yearning that's running untold
The phases of my life down in the place
A place I thought I never knew
Only to and fro from the past I never beheld
Troddening journeys to a place anew
Within the great confines an evening runs amuck
And towards the sinful coming days
I find a newfound glory that's routinely struck
And all along I've known the deep great truth
The one I have yet to behold with memories and stories so uncouth
Tomorrow is a better journey through the week
Seeping through the windows of my tired solemn soul
Deep within my loving great sorrows
I seek a yearning that is about to superficially unfold
The phases of my very existence
Trodden in a land I once thought I bluntly knew
Only to behold a past and future of phases and places
That are not what they used to be, were once brand new
The fun times forth a comin'
A great presence runs through my confused tattered mind
The thing so down in a place I only sought through
So solemnly in a place I could not hide seek or find
Where I could not speak or exist just a few
Tomorrow is a better natural beautiful year
Seeping through my tired withered soul
And with the time I lost, I've gained
a whirlwind of confusion and tetherment my heart only knows
and with it all comes down a crashing
the great struggle to freedom I can only hope

The Land's Place

The land's place is a time of hope
A wondrous place where beauty only exists
The goodness brings forth time's love no doubt
The time that the sorrow brings within
A world where we hoped only for peace
But only found a place of distress and confusion
The places of hope and sorrow downtrodden in loathsomeness
Shattered and torn within the hopes of a winding troddenness

The Night's Journey

The place I sit to and forth a journey I undergo and undertake
I sit and reflect on its very presence a creation I find so jubilant
And with it comes a humming noise, I broom broom the pedal to and fro
The placement of my hands, smirking smiles generated and inside I just say go
Fun joystick, I pull through while speeding through the night
Sitting down my winters night, the snow melting callously
Allowing me to make my way my short-lived journey through the slippery road
The lights bright seeping through, my eyes land upon a forest green jumping toad

Oh how she thanked me
Oh how she thanked me! She saw me walking down the road
I saw her come up to me utterly confused and wondering what was to come
Watching me throughout the still dark night
Acting as if I was a thankless pallbearer
Someone who barely cared about her or had no thoughts about the situation

Riddling the joystick with my exalted right hand
I run amuck the town all day and all night
Speeding to and fro down the streets of the place I exist and live
Having fun at the expense of the moonlit stars of the night
Rushing down the roads, bright lights comin' from afar
I hail to myself, it is the beautiful place I exist never to really go
The night's journey, began from a touring the radio's songs
And ended towards a land I journey to often
A nearby diner where I can sing my songs along

The Truth I Bear Will Never Be Known

Deep within it resides within heartfelt secrets cramped deep below
It once existed only to serve the purpose of destruction and hate
Changing the lives and futures the embolden hands of time and fate
Whilst those living their careless lives in ignorance and beautiful lack of knowledge
Exist without experiencing tragic injustices and hate
The truth I bear exists in a place unresolved
Seeking out healing and crying for the burdens to be taken and gone
Distant memories so close as if they were a split second ago
A traumatized existence only screaming and calling out for healing and passerbys to acknowledge and to behold
The truth I bear was once a severe and extreme burden
Only to rip apart a soul full of energetic bliss hope love and light
Hidden still deep within a world confined serving to exist
As that same menace it always was to tear apart destroy and invade
It calls out to be aching for justice peace and resolution
Only existing in the same manner and format to achieve to steal and repurpose dreams and goals
Resolution it so seeks and one day will possess
Until then it embellishes constantly and repurposes itself seeking destruction and being a menace
I journey far and even more distant Hoping for it to be resolved
Only knowing and coming across unlimited barriers and soul hampers
The truth I bear will never be known, in lands far and too deep
It exists now only to wrap itself around
The sorrows of my journeys defeat
The truth I bear will never be understood
For they fail to recognize the situation I must so blatantly endure
Only assumptions that run amuck, strike abound
Tempting to bring me down within a mind's distant allure

In Peace I Speak To You

In peace I speak, respectively to you
Did you ever listen, were you ever near
Or were you only ever pretending?
I thought I knew your deep dark heart
I thought I felt through the place you were hiding
But little did I know, you had no clue who you yearned to be
Only the person that hid deep within inside of me
Speak to me, did you ever know?

The pieces of me surrounding you that you tossed aside
The places within my soul withering away
Surrounding my confusion, hatred and non-existent pride
 In peace I respectively speak to you
Did you ever try getting to know the real true me
The person hidden deep within
A cherished gem you failed to care to understand or perceive
In peace I respectively try to speak to you
Ive tried so hard these coming years
The difficulty only gets more uncertain, the angst too confusing
Hoping, wilting away for nothing but a response to ease my fears

The Light Workers Blessings

The light workers blessings are many and extend far towards the light of all beings
Blessing souls and allowing harmonious blessings within the journey and existence of others
The work done is for the sole benefit of the good of each and every soul
To grace its path is only about existing to create and allow love and light to flow through and within
They are the angels of this realm assisting to create spread and produce harmony if they can
Creating a wealth of abundance and blessings
Interjecting with stars and wavelengths of unlimited positive pure energy to encompass those who can't
A lightworker seeks to know the happiness others possess
So it can intricately bless them with their own abundance and love and create a world of peace
They shatter the disillusion of fear and inner turmoil and grief
Creating an abundance of beauty and peace replacing it with glory joy and light

The Deep Sorrow

The deep sorrow lies heavily within my jaded confused mind
So deep inside I cannot fathom the place within that it so resides
It aches and yearns with every goal and aspiration I try to set
Only bringing heartache and destruction with every attempt I try to beget
The deep sorrow I so feel will only try to thwart my hearts greatest desires
It comes forth to bring myself an aching heartache that my soul aspires
The sorrow that I know now, will never allow me to be free
It sticks to my very gut and counterpart making me ache for a way to be from it
My soul sits heavy hearted wondering how and where it all went wrong
Deepening saddening going mad for a way for my heart and soul to again be strong
I live and abide by rules that never existed in a world gone wrong
Dealing with situations and scenarios that no other human has had to be a part of
The deep sorrow I so feel will only try to thwart my hearts greatest desires
It comes forth to bring myself an aching heartache that my soul aspires
The sorrow that I know now, will never allow me to be fully free
It sticks to my very heart and counterpart making me ache for a way to be from it
My ladened burdened heart, yearning for an easy and steady way out
My shattered soul sits heavy-hearted, wondering how and where it all went wrong
Deepening saddening going mad for a way for a heart and soul again to be strong

Chapter 6:
My Soul That I So Cherish

Within My Soul Lies

I can only gain the powers of my blessings if I seek so within the powers of a deep sought reality
If I live in the comfort of existence they exist only to come rushing towards me
Within my soul lies a blessing I have yet to unravel
The powers that be deep within only taunt the caring nature that I've come to be
A soul can only go so far and then its treasures are stolen
It wishes to be sent towards the light with blessings and freedoms it once carefully has chosen
The world pushes me back and I move forth tearing through the bounds of madness
I can only fight this fight if I'm given the tools of truth and justice and light
In the inferno I chose to exist, and my existence has become a futile demise
If only I had wept and grieved for the treasures of that which I could not compromise
Sweet blessings to cherish and explore
The blessing we behold can only mask the truth of our true nature
Within My soul holds the lies of the beauty and tragedies untold
I faced a whirlwind of sorrows that the gifted never have to ever behold
Again I'm entranced in a situation where my destiny is grappling to unfold
Half-truths mark the mercy of the days that lie ahead
With a hidden past that encases hundreds of deep secrets I never want revealed or to tragically unfold
Predators lurk at every corner begging for my every wish and desire
Seeking only to damage and steal that which was once my beings true love and fire
Hidden wishes deep secrets taken from every corner of my existence
It lurks to steal the solace and comfort I possess and the gifts I consume towards justice

I can only grapple for the feat of my glory and hope that it stays far away
Yet by my presence it awaits and tramples seeking only to embrace and snatch more and more

Sweet Blessings I Once Possessed

Sweet blessings I once possessed stolen in a whirlwind of confusion and sorrow
Injustice reeks of my very blood and being in the grips of what I endure tomorrow
Sweet blessings taken and gone without a care in the world
When did it all go away, where did it all go wrong i grapple with the mystery of it all Who can I ask for some solace?
Love can be found within the secret light we bare the burden only too deep within
Existing within the blessings of a confined soul I grapple with the sorrow that sits and hovers within
Banishing the light that once shone bright
Extinguishing the gifts and mercies one by one
I seek to exist in a world full of justice and good where oh where did it all go wrong
The beauty that lies within was never meant to be confined
It was meant to spread its wings and rush free to a world full of love peace and pride

My Only Hope

My only hope is the place I once yearned for knew and explored
Journeying through the lands of time and knowledge accepting blessings from whomever I once knew
Gifts of fear and gladness peruse through my distracted mind
Trying to thwart the joy and bliss I seek within a world that can't be defined

I am the gift I seek within solace beauty and comfort that exist higher within
I am the love I so truly desire
Meant to exist in a reality with beauty and blessings that are deeper and higher
I only consume the selfishness of my own laid back life and good
Endless bounds of comfort and hope riddle my heart with goodness and love
If only I grasped the truth I always knew
Hidden deep within my core
Sweet blessings of light and hope deep that exist within
Would come pouring out into the existence of my soul
I am the gift I seek within higher comfort deep beauty of solace comfort and grace
The goodness I possess will always shine through and forth
Without allowing the negative and insipid to take place
I seek out the help and positivity that exists deep within the respite of my soul
Exacerbating the light within bringing forth unlimited bountiful blessings of hope and peace within a life of joy and light
The gift exists within me and finally I seek it out
Harboring blessings of goodness and oneness only to become more engulfed in its loveliness and hope

The Empath's Dream

The empaths dream is a gift of hidden mysteries untold
Dreams journeys pervasive boldness of beauty and creativity yet to behold
Sadness and sorrow transformed into joys and comfort
A soul desiring to exist solely to bless others with endless streams of love and light
A golden warrior set out to fight the battles of good versus evil
Living the life of freedom and justice yearning for the goodness that prevails
She seeks out only the gift of light and love
In a world where there is misery and drought evil and lack of hope
The gifts of the blessed and the blissful
Can only move forward within the realms of hope justice and truth
An empath works the world with its mysteries of empowering the system of good and blessing its sources with more positivity truth justice and grace
She is the mercy others so seek to
embrace and ask for help from
To mend their own tattered confused lives lost memories and forgotten journeys
The empaths gift is blessed within many worlds
As they cease to exist only to enlighten and benefit others and the planet
The work of angels they commit both near and far
Living in lands of joy and peace quick to extinguish any injustice hate or fear

Within My World You Disappeared

A souls purpose can only exist within the glimmer of hope and glory where dreams once resided
It seeks to encompass that which has faded away to bring forth journeys and experiences that seem to linger throughout and within
Fears and traumas writhing throughout hoping for deep resolution
That bring forth endless lessons meant to teach an amateur being the lessons of its truth spirit and journey
The blessings that exist within a boundless existence of light and pure energy encompassing vortices of love and truth
To cherish and create special goals and dreams that remain mysteries within the minds hidden eye
A souls purpose can only be revealed
Within the higher self of the gifted light creation that exists only as a containment of love and goodness
Trickling through the secret lessons designed to reveal the inner core of a special light beings true spiritual and soul lessons and existence
A souls purpose must remain intact and hidden and be slowly immersed within the mind of the special child it is meant to bless
Only to bring forth blessings and truths in order to create multiple experiences of joy and mystery throughout

Those Who Destroy

Those who destroy do not know yet they seek
The harm to those they can only because they believe they are helping their shattered broken inner selves
Confused and sorrowful souls full of misery and lack of mercy
They roam the land in lack of bliss and a state of inner hate confusion and endless misery
Unknowing of the demons they present inside
Possessing no knowledge of the chaos and destruction they create and ensue
Evil is their very core within their name
Ignorance and sickness consumes their souls while they run around with no shame
Those who destroy seek to harm the most innocent
The callous and the crude they run amuck, astray
Seeking only to ruin those who exist in innocent and goodness
Unworried about the treasures they take, the beautiful blessed days
Those who destroy, a thing in the world they never cared for
The beauty the great possess, they yearn to brutally snatch away
Only concerned with what their sorrowful hearts desire
Unaware of the sorrow and lamenting they cause the good victims

I Think I Know You Now

I think I know you now, for once I almost did
Thinking, hoping that maybe you existed in a land I held dear
Writhing to and fro, for the gracious times I caused you confusion
Bellowing softly, for the indignations you showed me all too clear

You aren't the person I once knew, the creation so sweet and genuine
A person I felt was the one true savior of good, the one who knew the ways
A gracious, humble kind soul who believed in good versus evil
Just like me, the fighting warrior for the greatness of all of humanity

I think I know you now, for once I thought I possibly knew you
You're the lackadaisical creature who seemed to care for all those times
You confessed and poured your heart's nature out to my soul
Only to confuse an already distraught person and languished fool

I think I know you now, but I maybe im totally wrong
I thought you had me fooled somewhere deep within my trodden self
But now you have another fooled, caught in your cobweb of traps
Into the abyss of life and nature, you exist and dwell

www.ingramcontent.com/pod-product-compliance
Lightning Source LLC
LaVergne TN
LVHW012047070526
838201LV00082B/3845